Andrea Helena Gruber

Munich´s History and Stories

Your self-guided walking tour through historic Old Town

Andrea Helena Gruber

Munich´s History and Stories

Your self-guided walking tour through historic Old Town

Publisher: BoD · Books on Demand GmbH, Überseering 33, 22297 Hamburg, bod@bod.de

Print: Libri Plureos GmbH, Friedensallee 273, 22763 Hamburg

ISBN: 978-3-8192-6563-1

Greetings from the Author

Dear guests,

I warmly welcome you to my hometown Munich, the capital of the state of Bavaria.

The Bavarians' slogan is *Mia san mia* and we really are what we are:

at times little loners and sometimes stubborn, very tradition-conscious, occasionally a bit grumpy, but with our hearts in the right place - on the whole, we are quite a nice bunch.

In addition to other local peculiarities such as brass music, *dirndls* and *lederhosen*, we have our own dialect, which is similar to the Austrian one. However, we roll the 'r' like Italians and Spaniards do, for example.

The Bavarian greetings, which our Austrian neighbours use in exactly the same way, sound very pious. But they do not necessarily provide any information about the religious beliefs of those greeting each other, although the majority of people living in the state of Bavaria are indeed Catholic.

Therefore, Bavarians greet each other with a formal *Griaß Gott* or an informal *Griaß di / eich* and say goodbye with a *Pfiat Gott* or *Pfiat di / eich*.

You can also address each other in a very familiar way with a *Servus* (from the Latin *at your service*).

Whether you want to use these pious greetings yourself is up to you.

I hope that my little digression has put you in the mood for your self-guided tour and I wish you a lot of fun. Or as we say in good Bavarian: *let's go – Gemma!*

Yours, Andrea Helena Gruber

Foreword

In Bavarian, *Schmankerl* means culinary treat.

The ten *treats* that you can explore yourself on my two-hour tour are historical and cultural highlights that are indispensable when visiting Munich's Old Town.

It's best to start at Marienplatz, the *heart* and center of Munich (*Treat 1*).

And if you've really had a pleasant taste for it, you shouldn't miss out on the five *extra treats*.

For those interested in history, the chapter on the Wittelsbach dynasty comprises the rulers who gave Munich its special charm with their love to construct buildings.

And the crowning glory is eating real treats at Munich's central food market, the Viktualienmarkt (*Extra treat 4*).

Table of contents

===

Your 'treat' route through Munich´s Old Town

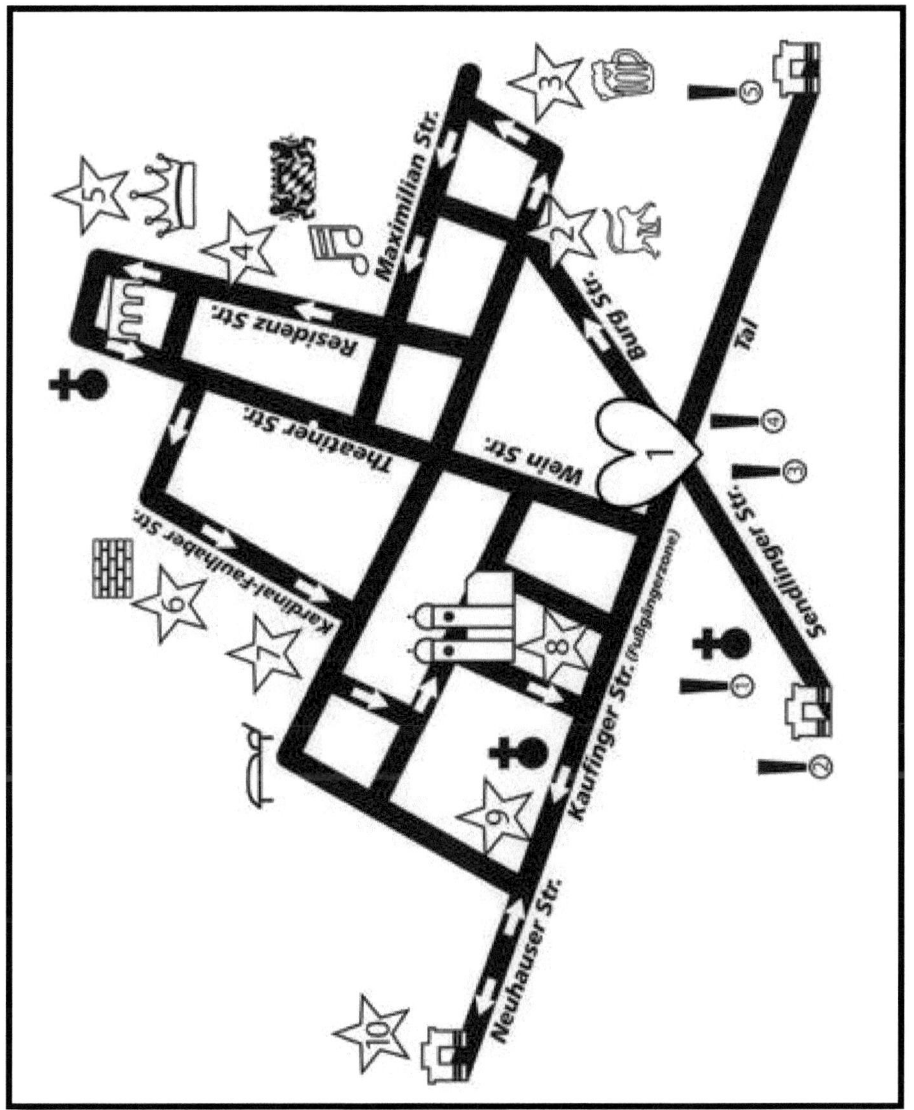

Marienplatz –
Here the *heart* beats and the carrillon chimes

Marienplatz is both the historical and geographical centre of the city.

Where numerous visitors flock today, there was a lively market and grain was sold until the middle of the 19th century.

In southern Germany, the grain market is also called the Schrannenmarkt. And that was the original name of the square.

At the same time, it was also the site where events, tournaments and even public executions took place.

When the market was moved in 1850 to the place where the Viktualienmarkt is today (*Viktualien* is the outdated term for food or groceries), it became the *stomach* and Marienplatz remained the *heart* of the city.

Marienplatz is named after the **Mariensäule**, which forms the exact geographical centre of the city. The column, and thus the entire square, is named after the golden statue of the Virgin Mary that stands on top of it.

The Mariensäule was erected in 1632 as a votive column during one of the worst and longest wars that Munich or Bavaria had ever experienced, namely the Thirty Years' War (1618 – 1648).

It stands there in gratitude that Munich was not destroyed during the Swedish occupation.

At the foot of the Mariensäule, four creatures fight the so-called *four plagues of humanity*, which is intended to symbolically show the connection between war and epidemics:

The snake stands for unbelief and refers to the Thirty Years' War, the lion represents the war itself, the dragon embodies famine and the basilisk stands for the plague.

For that reason, the Mariensäule later became a pilgrimage column, as people hoped that fervent prayers and offerings would bring about an early end to the deadly diseases. It was during a thanksgiving service to mark the presumed end of a cholera epidemic that Queen Therese, wife of <u>King Ludwig I</u>, became infected and died in 1854 as the last confirmed victim of cholera.

In the immediate vicinity of the Mariensäule is the **Fischbrunnen**, traditionally the venue where Munich residents arrange to meet at Marienplatz.

The central column of the fountain is decorated with a bronze fish, which is intended to remind people of the former fish market on Marienplatz and which also gave it its name. The three butchers´ boys who pour water into the fountain represent a centuries-old tradition according to which butchers´ apprentices celebrate the completion of their training every year on Shrove Monday by jumping into the Fischbrunnen.

This old ritual has been preserved to this day and still takes place every three years.

And every year on Ash Wednesday, the Mayor of Munich revives the tradition of the symbolic washing of a wallet in the Fischbrunnen, which is said to bring great financial blessings to the city.

But now let's move on to the most impressive building that dominates the entire Marienplatz and is often mistaken for the Munich Cathedral.

The Neues Rathaus (New Town Hall)

This oversized building in neo-Gothic style, on whose façade all members of the Bavarian ruling family (see <u>The Wittelsbach dynasty</u>) are lined up, houses a masterpiece of craftsmanship that is also one of the city's most famous tourist attractions:

The Glockenspiel (Carrillon)

daily at 11 a.m. and 12 noon, March – October also at 5 p.m. and 9 p.m.

365 days a year, two memorable events from Munich's past are brought back to life for about 12 minutes to the sound of bells:

To begin with, we see a colourful knight's tournament that was held on Marienplatz to mark the wedding of <u>Duke Wilhelm V, the Pious</u> and Renata of Lorraine. It was certainly one of the most extravagant and splendid festivals ever celebrated during the Renaissance.

After that, the Schäfflertanz takes us back to the time when Munich was ravaged by one of the four plagues, namely the plague. The *Schäffler* (barrel makers) went through the streets singing and dancing to lure the frightened people out of their homes and get the paralyzed public life going again.
The plague was finally overcome! This dance was and is still performed every seven years.

And last but not least, every day at 9 p.m. the **Münchner Kindl** is put to bed by the guardian angel and the night watchman, two of the 32 life-size figures.

Münchner Kindl

The Munich city coat of arms bears the diminutive form of a Benedictine monk, who gave Munich its name.

When the Huns were causing havoc in Bavaria in the 5th century AD, some Benedictine monks left their home monastery in Schäftlarn.

They fled downstream along the Isar river and founded a monks' settlement on the site of today's Munich, which the locals called 'bei den Mönchen' (near the monks). This is where the name Munich comes from!

By the way: The **tourist information** and **public toilets** are located on the ground floor of the Neues Rathaus.

The southwest corner of the Neues Rathaus is also called **Wurmeck**, which, like the Mariensäule, lies on an energy or dragon line between Peterskirche and Frauenkirche.

The word *wurm* is the abbreviation of the Lindwurm, a synonym for the mythical dragon.

And this plague dragon was said to have brought the *Black Death* upon the people with its poisonous breath and to have lived in exactly this place.

This is just one example of the superstition that dominated the lives of the Bavarian population in earlier times.

The **Altes Rathaus** (Old Town Hall) in late Gothic style is the work of the architect Jörg von Halsbach, who also built the Frauenkirche (Munich Cathedral).

Due to its *new* appearance, it is often confused with the Neues Rathaus, but it actually dates back to the 15th century.

However, after the entire destruction during the Second World War, it had to be completely rebuilt.

The tower now houses a toy museum, and in earlier times the first floor of the building accommodated a dance and banquet hall.

The city prison and the torture chamber were located in the northern part of the building, at the point where gate towers now lead pedestrians into the street of the Tal.

On the side of the Altes Rathaus and on the way to the Viktua-lienmarkt, there is a very popular statue commemorating the famous lovers Romeo and Juliet.

The **statue of Juliet**, a copy of the original statue in Verona, was a gift from the Italian community to its twin city Munich in the 1970s.

In contrast to the tragic end of the lovers, touching Juliet's breasts, as is the tradition with the original in Verona, is supposed to bring luck in love. This also explains her slightly rubbed off right breast...

However, as a 'compensation', she receives more flowers than any other woman in the city!

The **Peterskirche** (St. Peter's Church)

Locally and affectionately known as the 'Oide Bäda' (Old Peter), this church pales in comparison to the magnificent backdrop of the Neues Rathaus that stands opposite it.

Actually undeserved, because it is the oldest parish church in Munich, named after the apostle Peter, who is considered the first pope in history.

According to ancient custom, the tiara is removed from the altar figure of St. Peter every time a pope dies and is put back on when a new pope is elected.

You can also climb the Peterskirche and the Frauenkirche for an admission fee. A more comfortable option is to take the elevator up to the Neues Rathaus.

In any case, you will have a beautiful view of Munich's Old Town from the top of all three buildings.

Let's now continue towards **Burgstraße** with the oldest townhouses in the city.

Particularly worth mentioning is house number five, the **Weinstadl**.

The oldest and most beautiful Gothic townhouse was built in 1525 for the wine trade and storage. From 1552 to 1612 it served as the town clerk's office and was then returned to its original purpose.

The Weinstadl is also the prime example of an old Munich townhouse in the Ohrwaschl style. *Ohrwaschl* refer to the two gables with half-dormers that resemble a pair of ears. In the right *Ohrwaschl* there is still a cable winch that was used to pull the goods up into the storeroom.

Right next door, at number seven, the musician and composer **Wolfgang Amadeus Mozart** lived for a short time in 1780.

He composed his opera Idomeneo here, which was later premiered in the Munich Opera House. However, despite repeated requests, he was denied a permanent position at court.

François Cuvilliés (1695 – 1768), one of the great Rococo architects in Bavaria, lived and died opposite the Weinstadl. He designed the Cuvilliés-Theater, parts of the Residenz and Nymphenburg Palace, and much more.

Alter Hof –
'Monkey business' in the first duke's castle

The Ludwigsburg, as the **Alter Hof** (Old Court) was formerly called, was built in 1253 by <u>Duke Ludwig II, the Severe</u> and became the first city castle of the Wittelsbach dukes in Munich.

The construction of the second city wall led to the loss of the strategically important peripheral location of the fortress.

That's why in 1385, following a civil rebellion, construction began to create a kind of refuge against the incited mob. The result was the so-called *Neuveste*, today's Residenz.

Until 1508, court was held in both residences, which were connected by a corridor with the nearby Franciscan monastery.

Only after the final move to the *Neuveste* was the Ludwigsburg renamed Alter Hof.

In 1589, <u>Duke Wilhelm V, the Pious</u> laid the foundation stone for the court's first brewery.

From then onwards, brown beer had been brewed in the Alter Hof and for good reason:

Wilhelm V was fed up with having to import high-quality beer from northern Germany at great expense. He therefore decided to build his own brewery to supply the Wittelsbach family and their staff.

In 1808, the brewing operation in the Alter Hof was finally discontinued, after brown beer brewing had been gradually incorporated into the Bräuhaus am Platzl, today the world-famous Hofbräuhaus.

The wild monkey and the baby

The Alter Hof was also the birthplace of the later <u>Emperor Ludwig IV, the Bavarian</u>, where a tame monkey was kept as a pet.

*And this is how the story of the **Monkey Tower** came about:*

When Ludwig was still a baby, the monkey always jealously watched the nanny who took the little one out of his cradle and cuddled him.

One fine day, the monkey could no longer hold back and snatched the baby from the nanny who screamed in protest.

The wild primate had not expected so much resistance and fled, with the infant under his arm, to the highest tower of Ludwigsburg, later known as the Monkey Tower.

The entire court gathered and laid out pillows and mattresses under the tower in case the monkey dropped the baby.

Finally they managed to persuade it to return little Ludwig safely to his cradle.

It remains unclear whether that monkey or the tower really existed at the time. But in any case, it is a beautiful story!

As we leave the Alter Hof, we pass an equestrian statue of the former emperor, who fortunately survived the 'monkey business' at the tower.

On the way to our next *treat*, there is a building on the left with an entrance gate that is usually closed.

With a bit of luck, we can take a look into the arcade courtyard of the **Old Mint**, one of the most beautiful courtyards in the style of the German Renaissance.

Founded in 1567 as a stable and art chamber, the building housed the Royal Mint from 1807 and has been the seat of the Bavarian Office for Monument Preservation since 1995.

<table>
<tr><td>3</td><td>Platzl –
Beer enjoyment in the former red-light district</td></tr>
</table>

Munich's oldest square, the **Platzl**, is dominated by the world-famous and often replicated **Hofbräuhaus**.

The building in the neo-Renaissance style has a main guest room, the Schwemme, as well as various rooms for private events and a souvenir shop. It can accommodate up to 3,500 guests.

The excellent Hofbräu beer can also be enjoyed in the cozy beer garden in the inner courtyard.

The predecessor of the Hofbräuhaus was the Weiß-Bräuhaus, into which the brown beer brewery of the Alter Hof was gradually incorporated.

In 1828, the benevolent <u>King Ludwig I</u> approved public serving, thus giving the common people access to the court's brewery; a privilege that had previously only been reserved for the court. As expected, there was a mass rush to the brewery, which was soon completely overcrowded.

A larger new building was required, which is why the Weiß-Bräuhaus was demolished in 1896 and replaced by the current Hofbräuhaus.

In 1897, brewing operations were finally stopped here and initially moved to what is now the Hofbräukeller in Haidhausen, and later to the branch in Riem.

The former brewery was converted into the Schwemme, which today has room for around 1,000 guests. The word *Schwemme* also refers to halls in which beer is served in large quantities.

For a long time, the Platzl was firmly in the hands of the star chef **Alfons Schuhbeck**.

He ran a restaurant, shops for spices and tea, an ice cream parlour and even a cookery school here.

But this is a thing of the past, his businesses have either changed hands or will close soon. Tax evasion and his imprisonment in Landsberg am Lech in 2023 'broke his neck'.

The area around the Hofbräuhaus was considered Munich's red-light district until the early 1970s.

On the occasion of the 1972 Summer Olympics, the city was to be cleared and ridden of vice. The Munich pop group Spider Murphy Gang sang about the city fathers' clean-up operation with the title 'Skandal im Sperrbezirk'.

Every die-hard Oktoberfest visitor knows the lyrics of the song and can sing along loudly: 'There is a Hofbräuhaus in Munich, but brothels have to go ...'

That´s why it is also called 'liquid bread'.

For a long time, the price of beer was seen as a political barometer, and any increase in price was interpreted as an unmistakable sign of bad times or even heralding war, thus causing great uproar among the population.

The most famous was the Munich Beer Revolution of 1844, triggered by a price increase of one penny per liter.

In order to prevent an escalation, the king gave in and lowered the price of beer, and the angry crowd calmed down again.

There were and are many arguments that still speak in favour of beer consumption today:

When Munich was hit by epidemics such as the plague or cholera, beer was considered the only safe drink for a long time. By boiling it and together with its high alcohol and carbon dioxide content, beer was practically germ-free, which could not be said of the drinking water at the time.

Beer has been amongst the healthiest drinks with its approximately 2,500 ingredients, including almost all B vitamins, calcium, magnesium and phosphorus. The hops it contains not only have a calming but also an antioxidant and anti-inflammatory effect.

No wonder that around 1900 every Munich resident was said to have consumed an average of 1.5 litres of beer a day.

Over the years, however, more and more Munich beer cellars fell into disrepute, being misused as a venue for political and demagogic mass events.

For example, Adolf Hitler's failed beer hall putsch began in the Bürgerbräukeller in 1923, where the unsuccessful assassination attempt on Hitler by Johann Georg Elser was later carried out.

Therefore it´s not surprising that the later occupying power, the USA, viewed Munich's beer culture as closely linked to National Socialism and prohibited even the few undamaged breweries from producing beer until 1948.

From Platzl we continue and turn left into **Maximilianstraße.**

This is the most expensive shopping street in Munich, with many designer shops and the luxury hotel Vier Jahreszeiten. The street was also home to the boutique of the flamboyant and extravagant fashion designer Rudolph Moshammer, known as *Mosi* for short, who was strangled to death by a callboy in 2005.

The façades on Maximilianstraße named after <u>King Maximilian II</u> are designed in the so-called Maximilian style.

He created this unique architectural style, which combines pointed arches and elements from the neo-Gothic and neo-Renaissance periods, in order to clearly distinguish himself from the neoclassical style of his father, <u>King Ludwig I</u>.

At the end of Maximilianstraße we reach Max-Joseph-Platz, but before we devote our attention entirely to this ensemble, let's take a look back.

In the distance we see a free-standing building, the **Maximilianeum**, a royal foundation by King Maximilian II with the purpose of supporting particularly talented students from Bavaria and the Palatinate, including former Prime Minister Franz Josef Strauß.

Today the Maximilianeum is the seat of the Bavarian State Parliament, which pays an annual ground rent to the foundation.

Max-Joseph-Platz –
Splendour and magnificence in the new kingdom

Until 1803, there was a Franciscan monastery here, which was demolished during the secularization to make way for an impressive square, **Max-Joseph-Platz**.

The man who gave the square its name sits enthroned in the middle of it: <u>King Max I Joseph</u>

The monument was actually supposed to be unveiled on the occasion of his 25th anniversary in power. However, the first Bavarian king was not at all happy with the way the design was depicted.

After all, he wanted to be honoured in a majestic pose and not 'as if he were sitting on a chamber pot' as the monarch originally put it.

Max Joseph's resistance only lasted until his unexpected death, whereupon his son and successor, <u>King Ludwig I</u>, implemented the original plans against the wishes of his deceased father.

But Max I Joseph was to have the last word, because the first cast of liquid ore exploded shortly afterwards.

The monument was therefore not completed until ten years later.

A similar fate, as the result of a devastating fire, befell one of the two imposing buildings that adorn the square:

The **Nationaltheater** or Opera House, which is why the square is also known as **Opera Square**.

After the closure of the first *Electoral Opera House* on Salvatorplatz in 1799, Max I Joseph had the *Royal National Theatre* built on this square based on the model of the Théâtre de l'Odéon in Paris.

Today, the Nationaltheater is the main venue of the Bavarian State Opera and the Bavarian State Ballet and, with around 2,500 square metres and a capacity of around 95%, ranks among the largest opera stages in the world.

Many opera pieces by the composer Richard Wagner were premiered here.

Let us now look at the **Königsbau** (King´s tract) of the **Residenz**, to the left of the Nationaltheater, which was commissioned by <u>King Ludwig I</u> based on the models of the Palazzi Pitti and Rucellai in Florence.

From the middle of the square, it is difficult to imagine the gigantic size of the Residenz.

With an area of over 40,000 square metres, it is considered the largest German city palace and, with more than 150 exhibition rooms, is one of the most important palace museums in Europe. The associated **treasury chamber** is world-famous and today boasts more than 1,200 individual items.

The origin of the entire Residenz complex was the construction of the *Neuveste*, initiated in 1385. After the final move from the Alter Hof in 1508, it served as a city palace for all Bavarian dukes, electors and kings until 1918.

It is hard to imagine that after the bombing in the Second World War, barely 50 of the 25,000 square metres of roof area remained.

===

As you you walk from Max-Joseph-Platz along the Residenz, you will reach *treat 5*, the Odeonsplatz. And before that you will inevitably pass the famous bronze lions.

Since an anecdote from the time of <u>King Ludwig I</u>, these are considered to be good luck charms if you stroke their snouts.

The love-sick king and the bronze lions

The bronze lions are associated with one of the most spectacular love affairs of the 19th century.

A young Irish-Scottish impostor, who passed herself off as a Spanish dancer named Lola Montez, had completely turned the head of the then 60-year-old <u>King Ludwig I</u>.

And managed to turn the whole of Munich against her in less than 16 months.

In his love frenzy, which we would probably attribute to a midlife crisis today, the king appeared in public with 'his Lola', thereby humiliating his wife Therese, who was extremely popular with the people. He also included the dancer in his will and raised her to the nobility.

The king not only incurred the displeasure of the social elite from the church, politics and economy. His unpleasant relationship was also met with rejection in academic circles, which is why some students wrote defamatory letters and distributed them throughout the city.

The monarch was understandably 'not amused' and promptly offered a reward for the capture of the 'unknown perpetrators'.

One of the students made a joke out of it and designed a poster that he placed directly on the Residenz building: 'Unknown perpetrators? There were four of them: me, ink, pen and paper'. This brazen act led to his immediate arrest and he was consequently brought before the king.

But the humorous Ludwig was so impressed by the student's courage and wit that he not only pardoned him, but also gave him the reward that was on his head.

The student got away with a 'black eye' and, completely relieved, stroked the snout of one of the four lions as he left the Residenz.

Since then, the bronze animals have been considered to bring good luck and many passers-by cannot resist stroking the lion snouts at the bottom of the shield as they walk past - that's why they shine so beautifully!

<table>
<tr><td></td><td>

Odeonsplatz –
A piece of Italy in front of two generals
</td></tr>
</table>

If **Odeonsplatz** reminds you of an Italian piazza, it is primarily due to the following three striking buildings that characterize it:

The **Theatinerkirche**, the **Feldherrnhalle** and the **Siegestor** which is about a kilometre away. All of them were built based on Italian models.

The square bears the name of the concert and ballroom Théâtre de l´Odéon, which was located behind the equestrian statue of <u>King Ludwig I</u> and is now the seat of the Bavarian Ministry of the Interior.

The beautiful **Theatinerkirche** is the first Baroque church in Italian style north of the Alps.

It was built as a votive church in response to a vow after the long-awaited birth of the heir to the throne, <u>Elector Maximilian II Emanuel</u>, in 1662.

The marriage of his parents, <u>Elector Ferdinand Maria</u> and <u>Princess Henriette Adelaide of Savoy</u>, had remained childless for years despite all attempts.

It was only thanks to the active support of the Princess' personal physician (!!) that offspring in the form of a daughter was announced ten years later, which was little cause for joy.

But in 1662, the male heir to the throne, Maximilian Emanuel, finally saw the light of day. In order to express her boundless gratitude by founding a new church, the Princess brought monks from the order of the Theatines and architects from her home country of Italy to Munich.

The Theatinerkirche bears the name of said order and was built based on the model of their mother church, Sant' Andrea della Valle, in Rome.

The Princess was the first to find her final resting place in the princely crypt of the church. It is the most important of the three burial places of the Wittelsbach dynasty, alongside Michaelskirche and Frauenkirche.

Until 1817, the fourth of three remaining city gates, the Schwabinger Tor, stood in place of the two flagpoles on the square in front of the church.

The no longer preserved Theatinergang, a walk which ran high up along the former city wall, connected the Residenz with the church and the nearby Salvatortheater on Salvatorplatz.

Ludwigstraße, named after King Ludwig I, became Munich's first boulevard.

It links two buildings whose three round arches correspond architecturally with each other:

the **Feldherrnhalle** and the **Siegestor**

The **Feldherrnhalle** was built between 1841 and 1844 on the orders of King Ludwig I, and modelled on the Loggia dei Lanzi in Florence, as an entrance to the Old Town.

It is dedicated to the Bavarian army and two main figures in Bavarian military history, whose bronze statues are located under the left and right arches:

Count Tilly, general in the Thirty Years' War and Count Wrede from the Napoleonic Wars.

Both were mocked, the first not being a Bavarian and the second not being a general.

In the middle, a staircase leads to the army memorial in memory of the Franco-Prussian War of 1870, which is flanked by two marble lions.

The Feldherrnhalle gained notoriety through Adolf Hitler's attempted military coup on November 9, 1923 and his *march on the Feldherrnhalle*, which was ended bloodily by the Bavarian State Police.

After Hitler seized power in 1933, the Feldherrnhalle became a special place for National Socialist propaganda due to its highly symbolic character. Every pedestrian who walked past the monument had to give the Hitler salute.

If you wanted to avoid that, you had to turn into Viscardigasse from Residenz-straße, which is located behind the Feldherrnhalle, and you could then get to Odeonsplatz via Theatinerstraße.

Viscardigasse later became known as the *path of silent resistance* or, less flatte-ringly, as the *shirker's alley.*

The **Siegestor**, about one kilometre away, is the counterpart to the Feldherrnhalle with its three round arches.

It was built between 1843 and 1850 as a trium-phal arch based on the Arch of Constantine in Rome, with the addition of a crowning quadriga.

The patron saint of Bavaria, the **Bavaria**, steers a group of four lions.

The Siegestor commemorates the victorious end of the wars of liberation against Napoleon in 1815, but was destroyed in the Second World War.

After its reconstruction, the monument became a memorial with the following inscription: 'dedicated to victory, destroyed by war, a reminder of peace'

At number 13 Ludwigstraße is the Herzog-Max-Palais, where Elisabeth, later known as **Empress Sisi of Austria**, was born and grew up.

The Bavarian and the Prussian lion

The model for the two marble lions (the lion is considered as the Bavarian heraldic animal) was a big cat called Bubi from Munich's Hellabrunn Zoo.

Some Munich residents jokingly claim that one of the lions is of Bavarian origin and the other of Prussian origin. And how do you recognize the Prussian one?

It is the one that 'opens its big mouth', which is to be understood as a humorous allusion to the alleged talkativeness of the Prussians and as an expression of the animosity between Bavarians and the 'northern lights'.

A key reason for this lies in the 19th century, in the constant struggle for supremacy in the German Confederation, which ended in a civil war in 1866 and underlined Prussian superiority.

That war was primarily directed against Austria, but the defeat of the allies, Bavaria and Austria, brought the two neighbours even closer together in the fight against the strong enemy in the north, in addition to their similar dialect and mentality.

When Bavaria lost its sovereignty in 1871 with the founding of the German Empire, a further rift developed between the Catholic-dominated south and the Protestant north.

It is therefore not surprising that the Bavarians have a fictitious border, the so-called Weißwurst (white sausage) equator, whose course, geographically speaking, roughly corresponds to that of the Danube. Everyone who lives south of this border 'may' call themselves 'Bavarians', while the rest of the republic consists of the so-called 'Preißn'.

As a result, the old insult 'Preiß' or even 'Saupreiß' lives on in the minds of some stubborn Bavarians to this day. It has now become a general term for everything that comes from the north.

But perhaps despite or precisely because of the mutual taunts, the well-known saying 'those who love each other, tease each other' still holds true?

Salvatorplatz –
Greek flair beside the old city wall

Salvatorplatz is named after the **Salvatorkirche**, which served as the cemetery church of the Frauenkirche from 1480 until the end of the 18th century, when the burial site was moved to the Southern Cemetery outside the city fortification due to the risk of epidemics.

In 1829, <u>King Ludwig I</u>, who was a Greece enthusiast, handed the church over to the Greek Orthodox community.

The former cemetery, which was later turned into a market square, was used until 1906 as the site of the Greek market, a kind of second food market for farmers from the surrounding area.

The city's first opera house, the **Salvatortheater**, was located on Salvatorplatz.

It was built in 1657 at the instigation of the art and culture loving <u>Princess Henriette Adelaide of Savoy</u>.

The size of the Salvatortheater was not geared to the ever-growing opera audience, however, and so it was demolished in 1795 and the opera was moved to the newly built Nationaltheater on Max-Joseph-Platz.

The **Literaturhaus** has been located here since 1997 (entrance from the other side of Salvatorplatz).

The only clearly visible remains of the **old city wall** are located on Salvator-platz, which is why the Salvator-garage has been under monument protection as a supporting structure since 1964.

A sign here commemorates the for-mer **Maiden's Tower**, which was part of Munich's city fortification.

The late Gothic tower had always been a source of eerie feelings for the people of Munich since its construction in 1493 and they were glad when it was finally demolished in 1804.

The Kiss of the 'Iron Maiden'

*The **Maiden's Tower** had always been surrounded by gruesome legends.*

It was said to have been the seat of a secret council during the reign of <u>Elector Karl Theodor</u>. Citizens who followed revolutionary principles or did not suit the authorities were sentenced to death and executed there without a proper trial.

The name of the tower also gives rise to speculation.

With regard to buildings in Bavaria, the term 'maiden', 'virgin' or 'dear woman' usually refers to the biblical Virgin Mary. But in that case it had sup-posedly been an instrument of torture and execution called the 'Iron Maiden'.

It was rumoured, among other things, that those convicted had to kiss the statue of the maiden, the so-called 'maiden's kiss', and then fell through a trapdoor into a dark dungeon, where they then perished miserably.

Let us now walk along **Kardinal-Faulhaber-Straße** towards Promenadeplatz.

The houses of the nobility with façades in the Rococo style are particularly striking here.

The most famous aristocratic palace at number seven is the **Palais Holnstein**, which François Cuvilliés built in 1735 on behalf of <u>Elector Karl Albrecht</u> for one of his many illegitimate sons (the exact number is not known), the Count of Holnstein.

As the offspring of an elector, he not only claimed the name, but also the family coat of arms, to which, however, he was not entitled as an illegitimate child.

As a concession, the Bavarian electoral coat of arms was placed at the very top of the gable of the palace, but marked with a red line, the so-called *bastard beam*.

Interestingly, the Archbishop of Munich and Freising, currently Kardinal Reinhard Marx, comes and goes under this sinful beam every day.

The Palais Holnstein has been the Archbishop's Palace since 1821 and is therefore the residence and office of the high church dignitaries.

Promenadeplatz –
Much ado in the former aristocratic quarter

From the 14th to the 18th century, the salt warehouses were located on **Promenadeplatz**, the former Kreuzgasse.

Salt, which was one of the most valuable and sought-after goods at the time and came from Berchtesgaden and Bad Reichenhall, had to be stored in the city for a few days and offered for sale due to the *staple law* applicable in Munich. Only then could it be transported further.

Due to its proximity to the Residenz, more and more nobles moved to the Kreuzviertel in order to get into the orbit of the ruling elite.

However, the *blue bloods* soon felt bothered by the loud hustle and bustle around the salt market and at their instigation, the salt warehouses were moved to Arnulfstraße near the main train station at the end of the 18th century.

Thus the Kreuzviertel first became an elegant aristocratic district with a promenade square and later a banking district.

The most famous is the Hypobank, founded in 1835 by the royal family as the first bank with banknote privileges and integrated into the Bavarian Central Bank in 1871.

The *Royal Bavarian Branch Bank*, founded in 1869, became the Bavarian State Bank in 1918 and was taken over by the Vereinsbank in 1970.

The **Bayerischer Hof**, which dominates Promenadeplatz, was the first grand hotel in Munich under King Ludwig I, who visited the hotel twice a month because, unlike the Residenz, it had a bathtub.

The hotel is also the venue of the **Munich Security Conference** (Siko), which takes place every year in February.

With more than 450 participants, including high-ranking politicians from all over the world, it is considered the most important international forum for current security and foreign policy issues.

The adjacent **Palais Montgelas**, which has been part of the luxury hotel since 1969, was once the home and workplace of Count Maximilian von Montgelas.

We see his statue in front of the building.

From 1817 to 1933, the palace was used as an office building for the Bavarian State Ministry of Foreign Affairs and, during the Nazi era from 1933 to 1945, was the seat of the Bavarian State Chancellery (Bavarian government).

One of the most memorable events in Bavaria's democratic history took place on February 21, 1919, in the immediate vicinity of the palace.

After the Wittelsbach dynasty was deposed and the last Bavarian king, Ludwig III, fled, Kurt Eisner was the first Bavarian Prime Minister to proclaim the Free State of Bavaria in 1918, meaning *free from the monarchy*.

Tragically, just a few months later, he was shot dead on Prannerstraße on his way to the state parliament. He was about to hand in his resignation when the right-wing radical Anton Graf von Arco auf Valley ambushed him in the street and murdered him.

Today, the **Kurt-Eisner-Denkmal**, a floor slab with his outline at the corner of the Palais Montgelas, commemorates the site of the assassination.

Frauenkirche –
A pact with the devil

The most famous landmark of Munich are the outstanding towers of the **Frauenkirche** (Munich cathedral), which can be seen from far away and be used to orientate oneself.

This view goes back to an old law that limited the maximum height of buildings to 100 metres, which is the height of the two towers. That initially only applied to the city centre and was then extended to the entire city area in 2004 by referendum.

However, anyone who thinks that the shape of the two towers, named Stasi and Blasi, reminds them of female attributes and derives the name Frauenkirche (literally translated *woman´s church*) from that is completely wrong.

The name Frauenkirche is an abbreviation of Dom zu unserer lieben Frau and is dedicated to the Mother of God.

But the shape of the towers, the so-called *Welschen* (foreign) domes, is still unusual. They do not fit in at all with the late Gothic style of the church interior.

One explanation is based in its history:

After 20 years of construction (1468 – 88), the architect Jörg von Halsbach and those responsible ran out of bricks, and money as well. That is why after his death in 1488, construction was put on hold.

It was not until 1525 that the towers, which stylistically already heralded the transition to the Renaissance, were added by Lukas Rottaler.

The construction of the Frauenkirche was a result of the rapid population growth at the time and the fact that Munich's first parish church, Peterskirche, could no longer provide enough room for all worshippers.

Later it even overtook Peterskirche when it was elevated to a Cathedral, the seat of a bishop, so to speak. The current Archbishop of Munich and Freising is Reinhard Marx.

Inside the church, we can see a monument made of black marble, the **Imperial Tomb** containing the mortal remains of <u>Emperor Ludwig IV, the Bavarian</u>, and the **Devil's footprint**.

The Devil's footprint

In the forecourt of the church, the wind will blow around your ears even on calm days.

Today, this phenomenon can be explained scientifically in the case of tall buildings. At the time, however, it was assumed that there was a much more diabolical force at work, meaning the devil simply had to have a hand in it.

This is how the legend about the Devil's footprint came about:

When the Prince of Hell got 'wind' of the construction of a new church, he rode up on it to thwart the plans. It was not too late, as the Frauenkirche had not yet been consecrated.

The architect, however, was a cunning fellow. He made the devil himself promise not to destroy his church, in return he would not install any windows.

Of course, the architect did not keep to the agreement, but installed the windows in a way that the devil could not see them during his regular inspection visits.

Only after the church was consecrated did the devil realise that he had been duped. He became so furious that he stamped his foot on the spot from which he had been watching the construction progress, leaving his footprint behind.

Extremely angry, he stormed out of the church and simply left his companion, the wind, behind. It is said that his subordinate still waits for his lord and master in front of the church and blows hard.

The devilish footprint today corresponds roughly to shoe size 46 and, according to medieval beliefs, stepping over it freed one from negative energy and sins.

Michaelskirche –
Remains of the 'Bavarian Escorial'

The **Michaelskirche** (St. Michael´s Church) in the pedestrian zone is so well embedded in the street that it can easily be overlooked as you walk past.

Dedicated to the Archangel Michael, it is considered as the spiritual centre of the Counter-Reformation.

The founder of this church, <u>Duke Wilhelm V, the Pious</u>, was not given this nickname without reason as he was one of its most ardent supporters.

His image, together with a model of the church, is on the façade, surmounted by a figure of Jesus Christ with a globe, who watches over Munich's city centre as Salvator Mundi.

The Michaelskirche was built between 1583 and 1597 based on the model of Il Gesú, the Roman mother church of the Jesuits.

The central theme is shown on the outside of the church in the form of a bronze figure of St. Michael fighting Satan with a lance, an allegory for the victory of faith over unbelief.

The Michaelskirche ranks among the largest Renaissance churches north of the Alps with a monumental barrel vault, the second-largest free-standing barrel vault in the world with a width of around 20 metres.

The tomb of Wilhelm V and his wife Renata of Lorraine was originally planned in the choir area of the church, but for unknown reasons, it was never completed.

The decorative parts of the tomb are now spread across the entire Old Town of Munich: The statue of the Mother of God is found on the Mariensäule, the lions at the Residenz and the flag bearers at the Imperial Tomb in the Frauenkirche.

The Michaelskirche, together with a Jesuit monastery and a city palace, formed a building complex that was originally known as the *Wilhelminische Veste*, after Duke Wilhelm V, and later as *Maxburg*, named after his son Maximilian I.

At that time, the complex was regarded as the 'Bavarian Escorial' because its incredible dimensions could actually compete with the Spanish royal residence near Madrid.

Unfortunately, it was completely destroyed in the Second World War, and only the church and the Maxturm remain.

Our 'Kini', the fairytale king <u>Ludwig II</u>, has also been resting in the princely crypt of the Michaelskirche since his death in 1886.

A sign from the Archangel Michael

When the tower of Michaelskirche collapsed during construction in 1590, destroying the choir, the city council tried to convince Duke Wilhelm V, in view of his excessive building frenzy, to forego the choir area altogether.
They claimed that the collapse was clearly a sign from God.

The duke, in turn, interpreted the incident as a sign from the Archangel Michael to make it even larger in order to do justice to such an important angel as the latter.

And so, despite all the objections of his advisers, a disproportionately long choir area was created facing north.

Karlsplatz (Stachus) –
Square and gate of the unpopular Elector

The old salt route was called Neuhauser Straße because it ran towards the western district of Neuhausen.

It connected Marienplatz with Neuhauser Platz or Neuhauser Tor, respectively, and is now Munich's central pedestrian zone.

After <u>Elector Karl Theodor</u> had the old city wall torn down, the square and the gate were renamed **Karlsplatz**, respectively Karlstor, in his honour in 1792.

It was probably due to the unpopularity of the Elector of the Palatinate that the name never really caught on and the square is better known in everyday language as **Stachus**, after the indeed more popular innkeeper Eustachius Föderl, who ran his restaurant nearby.

Until the 1960s, Karlsplatz or Stachus was one of the busiest squares in Europe, hence the typical Munich saying *'it's just like at Stachus here'*, referring to places where there is a lot of activity.

It was only when the main U-Bahn and S-Bahn (metro and suburban railway) junction was expanded and moved underground for the 1972 Summer Olympics in Munich that traffic calmed down on the square.

That measure also ensured that Neuhauser Straße was converted into Germany's first pedestrian zone and can still be considered Munich's main shopping street today.

Asamkirche –
A Rococo church at private expense

From Marienplatz we turn into Rosenstraße, which leads into Sendlinger Straße, towards Sendlinger Tor.

The Sendlinger Straße is now part of the pedestrian zone and has been completely car-free since 2019. It was also a trade route that led via Sendlinger Tor directly to Marienplatz, the old market square.

A few hundred metres from the old city fortification gate is the **Asamkirche**, a true jewel of Bavarian Rococo, which, for once, was not named after a saint, but after its donors.

The Asamkirche was the private church of Egid Quirin and Cosmas Damian Asam, two important Rococo artists whose former home is adjacent to the church.

The foundation stone was laid at the Asam brothers' own expense in 1729, the same year in which the *bridge saint* and patron saint of confessional secrecy, John of Nepomuk, was canonized.

This vicar from Prague had refused to break the seal of confession at the urging of King Wenceslas, who accused his wife of infidelity. He was then tortured and drowned in the Vltava.

The silver tongue on the high altar and the five stars in its halo, which are interpreted as the five letters of the Latin word tacui (I have kept silent), are reminders of his courage and devotion to God.

The Asam brothers dedicated the church to St. John of Nepomuk, who, they believed, had saved them from misfortune.

They had previously been caught in a severe storm on their ship on the Danube and were spared through their pleading with the patron saint.

This event is also symbolized by a replica of Danube rocks located at the entrance to the church.

<table>
<tr><td>②</td><td>

Sendlinger Tor –
Former *quarter of executioners and whores*

</td></tr>
</table>

The **Sendlinger Tor**, first mentioned in documents in 1318, is one of the three remaining city gates.

Not far from here was the executioner's house with a tower top that, with a lot of imagination, looked like a clenched fist.

It was reported that on the evening of the execution of an innocent man, the tower glowed red and at the same time a ghostly hand knocked violently three times on the executioner's door.

It is easy to imagine that executioners and their families were not really popular.

Due to their *dishonest* profession, they had to live outside the city fortification, were not allowed to visit public baths, sit with other guests in pubs and could only socialize and marry within their guild.

Until 1433, the executioner's house also served as a brothel and place of gambling, so that executioners also worked as pimps and brothel operators.

In 1436, the municipal *Frauenhaus* (outdated word for brothel), today the main fire station, was built nearby. It was available to unmarried men without restrictions and with great openness. Only Jews and clergy were forbidden access.

The end of the *Frauenhaus* and all Bavarian brothels occurred during the reign of Duke Wilhelm V, the Pious, who, true to his nickname of *the Pious*, put an end to the dissolute behaviours and sent the last few prostitutes to the monastery.

Following tradition, this district, like the Platzl, was home to the red-light district of the post-war period.

Jakobsplatz –
Memorial of the Jewish faith

The **Jakobsplatz** is named after Munich's oldest monastery and the Catholic church of St. Jakob am Anger.

In 2006, the Jewish centre with the main synagogue Ohel Jakob, whose base is reminiscent of the Wailing Wall in Jerusalem, the Jewish community centre and the Jewish museum was established here.

The interior of the synagogue can be accessed either via a 32-metre-long under-ground passage from the Jewish community centre or as part of a guided tour along the *Walk of Remembrance*, in which the names of 4,500 Munich Jews murdered in Nazi concentration camps are mentioned.

The old main synagogue, which was located near Karlsplatz, was one of the first synagogues in Germany to be destroyed by the Nazis in 1938 and is now only commemorated by a massive memorial stone.

The **Münchner Stadtmuseum**, founded in 1888, is the largest municipal museum in Germany and shows almost everything you need to know about Munich.

It has been closed since the beginning of 2024 for general renovation.

The Marstallhof, one of the two courtyards, which are framed by four buildings and where the city café is also located, is well worth seeing.

Also worth mentioning is the **Ignaz-Günther-Haus**, the former home of the Rococo sculptor Ignaz Günther at St. Jakobs Platz 20.

Inside the building there is a *ladder to heaven*, which, along with the *Ohrwaschl* in Burgstraße, is typical for old Munich townhouses.

It is a steep staircase that, without changing direction, opens up all floors of the house and thus, apparently, leads directly to heaven.

With a bit of luck, the front door will be open and you can catch a glimpse of a typical Munich *ladder to heaven*.

Viktualienmarkt –
Exotic *stomach* of the city

The **Viktualienmarkt**, also known as the *stomach* of Munich, was established by relocating the Munich city market from Marienplatz, which had become too small as a place of trade.

From 1807 onwards it became a permanent market for food supplies, which were known in the southern German-speaking area as *Viktualien* (victuals).

But between 1823 and 1829 the newly created market had to be expanded due to lack of space. That included the demolition of the Heilig-Geist-Spital (Holy Ghost hospital). The exception was the **Heilig-Geist-Kirche**, which is one of the oldest surviving church buildings in Munich.

Before the invention of refrigeration technology, the market played a key role as a central location for supplying citizens with food and was open day and night. Today, the legal opening times in Germany apply.

The market stalls at the Viktualienmarkt were reassigned daily until 1870 and from then onwards became permanent.

In the 1950s, the bustling Viktualienmarkt developed into a gourmet market.

On an area of over 22,000 square metres, more than 100 traders offer fruit, vegetables, fish, meat, spices and delicatessen from all over the world.

The city's most central beer garden is also located on the Viktualienmarkt, and the beers from all six Munich breweries are served in rotation.

The market women's dance takes place here every year on Shrove Tuesday. This is the most famous event that the carnival in Munich has to offer.

The southern end of the market is bordered by the **Schrannenhalle**, built in 1852, which partially burned down in 1932 and served as a car park until it reopened in 2005.

From then onwards, numerous shops and restaurants shared the hall, and it was not until 2015 that a tenant for the entire hall was found: the Italian delicatessen chain Eataly, which opened its first German branch here.

Munich beer garden tradition

The areas around the shady chestnut trees, which were planted to cover the beer cellars to keep the beer cool in summer, had always been used as beer gardens. There you could enjoy the beer with some local bread.

However, more and more breweries also began to sell food, much to the annoyance of the surrounding restaurants which feared competition.

Numerous complaints from angry innkeepers led to a decree by
<u>*King Ludwig I*</u>*, who prohibited the breweries from serving food.*
Instead, from then on it was the brewery's beer and the snack from home.

Although this ban has long since expired, this beautiful and, above all, inexpensive tradition has been preserved to this day.

Isartor –
Entrance gate for the *white gold*

From Marienplatz we walk past the Altes Rathaus towards **Tal**, the former widest and busiest street in Old Town.

It ends at the **Isartor**, the last of the three city gates, which was built in 1337 as part of the major city expansion by <u>Emperor Ludwig IV, the Bavarian</u> and restored in 1833 in the neo-Gothic style.

Above the gate entrance on the outside of the Isartor there is a fresco depicting the triumphal procession after his battle at Ampfing in 1322.

The old salt road, which ran from Salzburg towards Augsburg, used to pass by that site.

Therefore, the old customs bridge over the Isar river, today's Ludwigsbrücke, was located very close by the later Isartor.

When crossing the bridge, customs duties had to be paid for the valuable commodity, salt, the so-called *white gold*. After all, it was not merely the only spice available, but was also used to preserve food, as a refrigerator replacement, so to speak.

Thus it can be concluded that a monopoly on the salt trade meant both immense wealth and power.

The Ludwigsbrücke played a decisive role in the founding of the city of Munich.

Duke Heinrich der Löwe (Henry the Lion) had previously snatched away the Bishop of Freising's rights to the market, coin and customs by destroying his bridge near Föhring and building his own customs bridge on the site of today's Ludwigsbrücke.

The resulting dispute was settled by Emperor Friedrich I Barbarossa in the so-called *Augsburger Schied* (Arbitration of Augsburg) on **June 14, 1158**.

The verdict confirmed the new customs bridge and awarded the bishop a third of the revenue.

This date has since been considered the **official foundation day of Munich** and a figure of the city's founder can be admired on the side of the Altes Rathaus facing the Tal.

You might also notice a clock on one of the towers of the Isartor that runs in the opposite direction, the hands of which are mirrored.

This is entirely intentional and a tribute to the German comedian and folk singer **Karl Valentin.**

In honour of him and his partner Liesl Karlstadt, the **Valentin-Karlstadt Musäum** with numerous bizarre exhibits and curiosities was opened in 1959 in the middle tower building of the Isartor. It is currently closed for renovation until probably 2026.

Part of the museum is the Turmstüberl curiosities café which can only be accessed with a museum ticket.

Karl Valentin – a leptosome with a lot of humour

Karl Valentin (1882 – 1948) was ahead of his time, a brilliant comedian and lateral thinker who made a name for himself as a result of his leptosome physique, such as his long, thin figure and distinctive nose profile.

This Munich original was also known as a real Munich grump and pessimist. With witty sayings such as 'I would have liked to like, but I didn't trust myself to allow it' or 'A stranger is only a stranger in a foreign land', he left a lasting mark on the Munich idiomatic language.

In the spirit of Valentinian humour, the museum named after him presents curiosities such as the proverbial nail on which he hung his carpenter's profession or a fur-trimmed winter toothpick.

The museum's visitor information is also characterized by its own humour.

For example, admission is free for 99-year-old persons accompanied by their parents, there is a family ticket for parents with children, married or unmarried, but without chewing gum and soda, and the museum can also be viewed from the outside free of charge.

THE WITTELSBACH DYNASTY

Below I would like to introduce you to some representatives of the Wittelsbach family who have left their mark on Munich's Old Town.

The Wittelsbach were originally the Counts of Scheyern from a community in Upper Bavaria, who moved their castle to Wittelsbach near Augsburg and from then on called themselves the **Wittelsbach**.

In 1180, Munich's city founder, the Welf **Heinrich der Löwe** (Henry the Lion), had his rights revoked and the fief transferred to Otto of Wittelsbach.

The Bavarian ruling house changed over time into the dynasty that ruled Europe for the longest time and without interruption: from **1180 to 1918**

The Wittelsbach started out as dukes, were allowed to call themselves electors from 1623 onwards, when Bavaria gained the right to elect (kings), and provided all Bavarian kings from 1806 until the end of the monarchy in 1918.

Duke Ludwig II, the Severe (1253 – 1294)

His nickname was almost a euphemism for the crime he was accused of.

Known as a very jealous and hot-headed ruler, he accused his first wife, Mary of Brabant, of marital infidelity and had her beheaded despite all protestations of innocence.

Shortly afterwards and unfortunately too late, it became clear that he had wronged her.

The people took that very badly and the church also demanded reparation, whereupon he founded the Fürstenfeldbruck expiatory monastery. He himself grieved over his actions for the rest of his life and, through his deep remorse, became one of the kindest and most lenient rulers of his time.

In 1253 he had the first residence of the Wittelsbach built in Munich, the **Alter Hof**, where his son Ludwig IV was also born.

Emperor Ludwig IV, the Bavarian (1328 – 1347)

Ludwig IV, who was born in the Alter Hof in 1282, was Roman-German king from 1314, an honour he shared with Frederick of Habsburg (double kingship), and **Emperor of the Holy Roman Empire** from 1328 onwards. The Munich city colours of black and gold stem from the imperial coat of arms.

The imperial coronation was preceded by a long feud with the papacy, resulting in the excommunication of Ludwig IV in 1324.

In 1328, however, the Roman people presented him with the imperial crown without involvement of the Pope, an outrage that subsequently earned him the derogatory nickname of 'the Bavarian'.

The **Imperial Tomb** in the Frauenkirche was dedicated to the first and only Bavarian emperor.

Among other things, we owe him the **construction of the old city fortification**.

Of the original four city gates, only three remain: the Karlstor, the Sendlinger Tor and the Isartor.

Duke Wilhelm V, the Pious (1579 – 1597)

Wilhelm V owes his nickname to his devoted attitude towards the Catholic Church. His piety made him one of the most ardent advocates of the Counter-Reformation.

In 1597 he abdicated in favour of his son Maximilian I who led Bavaria (as elector from 1623 onwards) at the head of the Catholic League throughout the Thirty Years' War (1618 – 1648).

Wilhelm V, the Pious, is not only depicted at his wedding in the **carillon** of the Neues Rathaus, but also as a figure on the façade of **Michaelskirche**, built in the spirit of his 'fight against unbelief'.

Elector Ferdinand Maria, the Peaceful (1651 – 1679) and Princess Henriette Adelaide of Savoy

In 1650, Ferdinand Maria was married by proxy to Henriette Adelaide of Savoy, who was the same age (both 14 years old), and who was actually intended for King Louis XIV.

This type of marriage through a representative, which was common at the time, took place in the absence of the bride and groom, which is why they only met two years later, when the bride finally arrived in Munich.

The fun-loving Henriette Adelaide not only brought the religious order of the Theatines to Munich, but also introduced Italian festivals, theater and opera, as well as art and culture from France.

Elector Ferdinand Maria paled somewhat next to his glamorous wife, but through his far-sighted alliance policy and neutral attitude he nevertheless achieved his life-long goal of peace for Bavaria, which is why he was nicknamed 'The Peaceful'.

Elector Maximilian II Emanuel (1679 – 1726)

In contrast to his father, Max Emanuel aspired to military and political fame.

His declared goal was to become king or emperor. With that in mind, he had the **New Schleißheim Palace** built in the north of Munich as his future residence.

His military career, which kept him away from Bavaria for almost half of his reign, earned him not only fame but also the honorary title of 'Blue Elector'.
That was due to the colour of his uniform, which he wore in the so-called *Turkish Wars* (1683 – 1699).

The Spanish King Charles II appointed Max Emanuel *Governor General of the Spanish Netherlands*, now Belgium, in 1691.

In the War of the Spanish Succession (1701 – 1713), however, Bavaria suffered a bitter defeat on the side of France against Austria, which forced Max Emanuel into exile once again.

Despite all his efforts, he was unable to gain the title of king or emperor during his lifetime. That success would later be attributed to his son, Karl Albrecht.

Elector Karl Albrecht (1726 – 1742) / Emperor Karl VII (1742 – 1745)

Karl Albrecht aspired to the imperial title, which he claimed after the death of the Habsburg Emperor Karl VI due to his marriage to Maria Amalia, one of the emperor's nieces.

Shortly after the outbreak of the War of the Austrian Succession (1740 – 48) against his opponent Maria Theresia (daughter of Karl VI), he became **Emperor of the Holy Roman Empire** in 1742 and remained Emperor Karl VII until his death, albeit without a power base in Bavaria.

Elector Karl Theodor (1777 – 1799)

When the Bavarian line of the Wittelsbach family died out with his predecessor Max III Joseph, the Elector of the Palatinate took over the fate of Bavaria.

He was never able to warm to the country and its inhabitants, and the feeling was mutual. After all, he had tried twice (1778 and 1784) to exchange Bavaria for another territory, most recently for the *Austrian Netherlands*.

Both attempts had failed, but the Bavarian people still resented him.

In domestic politics, he was liberal and progressive, for example, he abolished torture and had the old city wall torn down, of which only the **Karlstor**, named after him, remained, along with the Sendlinger Tor and Isartor.

He made parks and green spaces accessible to the public, such as the Nymphenburg Palace park or the court garden of the Residenz, which had previously been reserved exclusively for the ruling family.

With the founding of the **Englischer Garten**, a landscape garden in the English style, he gave his citizens one of the largest inner-city parks in the world.

Despite his benevolent gestures and deeds, he remained very unpopular with the people throughout his life, which ultimately resulted in the news of his death in 1799 sparking public applause.

Elector Max IV Joseph (1799 – 1806) / King Max I Joseph (1806 – 1825)

The fact that Bavaria was elevated to a kingdom in 1806 and that Max Joseph became the first Bavarian king is due to the fact that Europe was dominated by the politics and conquests of Napoleon Bonaparte at that time.

In 1806 Napoleon founded the *Confederation of the Rhine*, a union of German states which consequently had to leave the Holy Roman Empire (of the German Nation), sealing its end.

In return, several principalities allied with Napoleon were elevated to kingdoms, including Bavaria.

The price to be paid was indeed high: 40,000 Bavarian soldiers died at Napoleon's side in the Russian campaign alone.

An obelisk on Karolinenplatz near the university honours the Bavarian soldiers who died in Napoleon's service.

King Ludwig I (1825 – 1848)

The second Bavarian king, Ludwig I, may not have the same level of fame and popularity as his grandson, the fairytale king Ludwig II, affectionately called 'Kini' by the Bavarians, short for king.

But Munich owes him a lot more in terms of architecture and culture.

Already as crown prince, he was enthusiastic about Roman and Greek antiquity, undertook numerous cavalier trips, including to Italy and Greece, and brought back ideas for boulevards, monuments, squares and buildings.

According to his vision, Munich should become an 'Athens on the Isar' and 'nobody should be able to say that they know Germany without having seen Munich.'

His passion for architecture led to the creation of many neoclassical buildings and boulevards, such as **Ludwigstraße, Odeonsplatz** with the **Feldherrnhalle** and the **Siegestor, Königsplatz** as a Greek forum, the **Königsbau** of the Residenz, to name just a few.

King Ludwig I was also a great asset to urban development in cultural terms.

Through his wedding to Therese of Saxony in 1810 and the associated celebration, in which the entire population of Munich was allowed to take part, the then crown prince initiated what is now the largest folk festival in the world, the **Oktoberfest**. It has since been held on the Theresienwiese, which was named after the bride, and is also popularly known as 'Wiesn' for short.

It was no secret that the king had a preference for beautiful women.

He had 36 beauties from all walks of life painted for his **Schönheitengalerie** (gallery of beauties) in the Nymphenburg summer palace.

And one of them would later cost him the throne.

We are talking about his unfortunate liaison with the young Irish-Scottish impostor Lola Montez, who posed as a Spanish dancer and ultimately became the trigger for his later abdication.

As *Countess Marie of Landsfeld*, Lola Montez increasingly interfered in political affairs, making her extremely unpopular not only with the people. Also the clergy and Ludwig´s own cabinet disapproved of their relationship.

Under that massive pressure, which was further exacerbated by student unrest, Ludwig I was forced to expel his mistress.

The monarch felt robbed of his royal power and dignity and saw the only solution in abdicating of his own accord, because 'I could no longer rule and I did not want to be merely a signee', he lamented.

King Maximilian II (1848 – 1864)

The son of King Ludwig I and father of King Ludwig II had a great love of science and would indeed have preferred to become a professor rather than king.

He intended to make Bavaria an intellectual and cultural centre with a role model function for the entire German Empire and was considered a patron of the arts, sciences and ethnicity.

He was convinced of the superiority of North German culture and the cultivation of the human science there, in stark contrast to his people, who considered the 'northern lights' to be arrogant, busybodies and know-it-alls.

Maximilian II, on the other hand, had a great affinity to Prussia, not least because his wife Marie came from the Hohenzollern dynasty there. He did not much like the Bavarian *seppeln* whom he considered to be simple-minded as well as ignorant and therefore wanted to provide them with sufficient education.

For that reason, he founded the collection for the **Bayerische Nationalmuseum** 'to honour and be an example for my people' and the **Maximilianeum**, a foundation named after him for the promotion of highly gifted students.

King Maximilian II is also considered a representative of the unique Maximilian style.

King Ludwig II (1864 – 1886)

And last but not least: Our 'Kini', the fairytale king Ludwig II.

Due to his fame and popularity, he should be mentioned here, although Munich cannot boast any buildings commissioned by Ludwig II.

His only contribution to urban development was the foundation of the *Polytechnische Schule* in 1868, today's **Technische Universität (TU)**.

The main reason for the monarch's lack of building activity was his deep aversion to the capital. He would have liked to *set fire to the city on every corner* and generally considered the people of Munich to be 'peasants', while they in turn secretly mocked their 'Mr. Huber', because insulting the Majesty was punishable.

When Ludwig II ascended the throne completely unprepared at the age of 18 years after the sudden death of his father, he was hopelessly overwhelmed by politics and court life.

At the same time, he was unable to sufficiently indulge in his true passions like art, theatre and music at court in Munich.

Therefore, he withdrew more and more from city life and created his own dream world in the Alps with his buildings, the **castles of Neuschwanstein, Linderhof** and **Herrenchiemsee.**

Closing Words

Dear guests,

We have now reached the end of your self-guided tour.

I hope you enjoyed your stroll through the Old Town, ideally under a blue and white sky, like the colours of the Bavarian flag, and were able to gather many new impressions.

Perhaps you have acquired a taste for it and next time I can personally show you my hometown at its best.

You can find more information on my website **www.visit-muc.de**.

I look forward to your visit and say goodbye with a warm farewell and

Pfiat Gott!

Yours, Andrea Helena Gruber